PULLING TOGETHER FOR COOPERATIVE LEARNING

Cooperative Learning Activities and Projects for Middle Grades

by Imogene Forte
and
Joy MacKenzie

Incentive Publications, Inc.
Nashville, Tennessee

Cover and illustrations by Cheryl Mendenhall

ISBN 0-86530-182-4

Table Of Contents

Preface

PULLING TOGETHER FOR COOPERATIVE LEARNING is a sparkling, integrated-curriculum collection of challenging experiences in cooperative learning. The format of organized, step-by-step procedures for both the teacher-directed and the independent student activities makes it success-oriented and user-friendly!

The goal of cooperative learning is to reinforce and sharpen skills required for working constructively in a structured group setting toward the achievement of a common goal. Today's corporate world is desperately searching for resourceful, self-directing personnel who are able to function cooperatively with their associates to achieve consensus, determine action, brainstorm, synthesize and implement ideas, and contribute to a synergistic excellence that is unattainable through independent means. PULLING TOGETHER FOR COOPERATIVE LEARNING is designed to prepare middle grade students to meet the demands of that kind of world! A strong selection of projects and activities in all curriculum areas helps students learn:

- to listen to one another
- to interact freely and openly without prejudice
- to express themselves orally in a clear, concise manner
- to critique ideas rather than people
- to develop interpersonal social skills
- to explore a broad spectrum of life experiences necessary for success in the job market, marriage, friendship, community, and family relations

Each lesson is presented either as a teacher-directed experience or a self-directed student activity. Attention to the following guidelines will ease implementation and enhance the cooperative learning process.

1. Remember that for middle graders, the optimum number of students per working group is 2 to 5.
2. Group students who can work well together, whose strengths complement one another, and who can learn from one another. (Change groupings often.)
3. Provide adequate working time and space.
4. Consider accessibility of materials; make it easy!
5. Give clear instructions; be sure each group understands its goals.
6. Constantly reinforce with students the principle process objective in cooperative learning – to make each student in each group responsible for the learning and achievement of all group members. The group succeeds only when every member of the group succeeds!

Teacher's Choice

Ask three teachers this question: "If you could keep only five words in the whole English language, which five would you choose?" Record their answers on this page from A TEACHER'S BOOK OF WORD TREASURES.

A Teacher's Book of Word Treasures

Form a group with four other classmates and share completed pages of treasured words. Discuss reasons you feel the teachers had for selecting these particular words to save. Then from all the individual lists, create one composite list of only 15 words. These should be the words your group judges to be the teacher's most treasured words in the English language. Use construction paper and your own creative flair to make a group poster to present the 15 chosen words to the entire class.

BONUS: Together the entire class may identify the single most treasured word in each of the following categories: nouns, verbs, and adjectives.

Name _____ Date _____

Which Is Which?

Look at each pair of homonyms in the center column. Decide which of the two is related to the word in the first column; then draw an arrow to it. Draw an arrow from the other word to the related word in the third column.

I	II	III
dessert	mouse mousse	mammal
music	phrase frays	fight
humor	rye wry	bread
armor	night knight	darkness
war	guerrillas gorillas	zoo
king	reign rain	water
bet	gamble gambol	frolic
breathe	air heir	princess
trees	suede swayed	shoes
ears	hear here	place
wrestler	muscles mussels	ocean
destructive	bomb balm	soothing
7 days	weak week	sick child

BONUS: Make up at least five of your own homonyms to add to the game. Invite two or three classmates to join you in creating a game that can be used by middle graders to sharpen vocabulary skills and increase word power. It may be a board game, a group game such as charades, or one of your own style. Use your lists of homonyms as the basis for the game. Ask your teacher to provide a time when games may be presented and "field tested" by the class.

Name _____ Date _____

Negative Feelings

Use just these small circular spaces to demonstrate your own personal, intimate response to four different kinds of feelings. Use a word picture, an acrostic, haiku, cinquain, simile, metaphor, cartoon, abstract drawing, color, or idea of your own. Be prepared to share and explain your responses in a small group session.

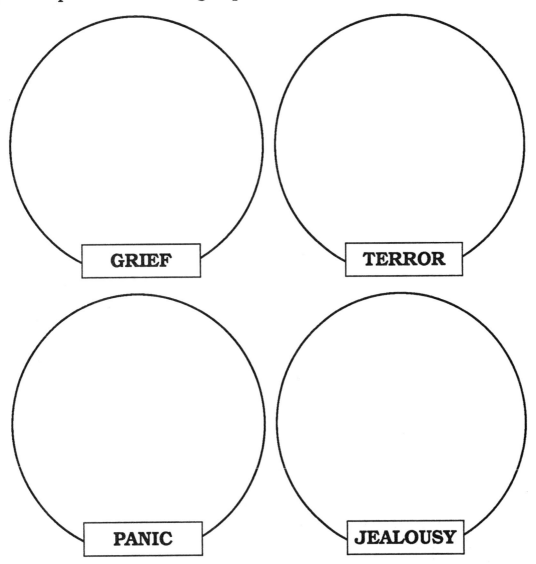

| GRIEF | TERROR |
| PANIC | JEALOUSY |

Meet in small groups to select one individual response which best represents each emotion as agreed upon by the the entire small group. (Warning: This could provoke lively discussion and decision-making!)

Name _____ Date _____

A Sight For Crossed Eyes

Page 1

Choose a working partner. Use the clues on the accompanying page to complete the crossword puzzle. You have been given only a few hints. See how much of the puzzle you and your partner can do in 25 minutes. Then stop and compare your progress with other pairs of partners in your class. Allow each pair of partners to ask for one further "hint" from classmates. Then complete the puzzle with your original partner.

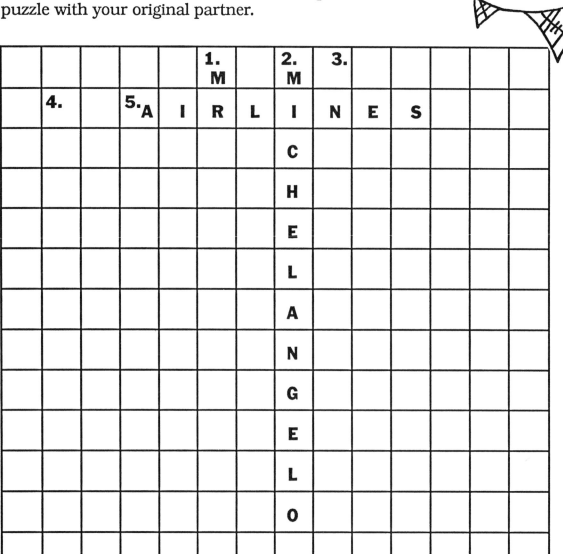

Name _____ Date _____

Language/Vocabulary, Spelling
© 1991 by Incentive Publications, Inc., Nashville, TN

*Answer Key

A Sight For Crossed Eyes

Page 2

ACROSS

2. Abbreviation for Miss or Mrs.
5. Delta, TWA, Air Canada
8. Not succeed
9. Expert combat flyer
10. Opposite of "she"
11. Negative answer
13. Between Lamentations and Daniel
14. Herb-flavored sparkling drink
15. Short for Edward
16. Law degree
18. Purity
21. Black gold
22. A pointed beard
26. Hot high
28. Greeting
30. Holy messenger
32. Affirm

DOWN

1. _____ and Mrs.
2. Famous Italian painter
3. Achoo!
4. Fence
5. Story with a moral
6. Sol, ____ te, do
7. Garment for mourning
11. Can't find in a haystack
12. No longer young
17. Prevaricate
19. Nimble
20. A, ____ , I, ____ , U
23. A continent
24. Skilled
25. Feminine for "he"
27. Past tense of "is"
29. For example (abbreviation)
31. Green light says, " ____ ."

Language/Vocabulary, Spelling
© 1991 by INCENTIVE PUBLICATIONS, Inc., Nashville, TN

Coded Communication

Page 1

Create a secret code that you have never used before. Cut out the three telegram forms on this and the other message page and use them to send a coded message to three of your friends. Send the identical message to each, and write the name of the receiver in the code on the line provided on each telegram form. (This will give the receiver the hint needed to "crack" your code.)

Deliver the telegrams to all three friends at the same time, and see which one decodes the message first!

TELEGRAM

CODED MESSAGE FOR: _____

MESSAGE: _____

_____

_____

_____

_____

_____

_____

_____

BONUS: The three friends must work together to create a coded message for you to solve!

Name _____ Date _____

TELEGRAM

CODED MESSAGE FOR: _____

MESSAGE: _____

_____

_____

_____

_____

_____

TELEGRAM

CODED MESSAGE FOR: _____

MESSAGE: _____

_____

_____

_____

_____

Language/Encoding, Decoding
© 1991 by Incentive Publications, Inc., Nashville, TN

Willy-Nilly Nomenclature

If you were not familiar with the Green Bay Packers, you might not guess that they were a football team. You might think they were a smoked fish market or a meat-packing company in Green Bay, or perhaps a large moving company.

Read this list of names that could have more than one identity. (You may make additions of your own.)

Twice Told Tales	The Ponderosa	Yugoslavia
Great Emancipator	Yellowstone	G.I.
Old Ironsides	Great Stone Face	Annapolis
Virginia Wolf	Pensacola	Old Glory
Headless Horseman	The Wizard of Oz	Big Ben
Stonehenge	Saskatoon	Istanbul
Babe Ruth	R.S.V.P.	A.F.L.
Hi Ho, Silver	C.O.D.	V.I.P.

Work in groups of two or three to choose five names. Write them in the first column below. Then give at least three identities to each. (One must be correct.) Exchange papers with another group, and try to make correct identifications.

1			
2			
3			
4			
5			

Name _____ Date _____

Language/Multiple Meaning, Word Play
© 1991 by Incentive Publications, Inc., Nashville, TN

Cranium Corporation

Read each of the following statements carefully. Then write an original "created by you" word to describe each.

a person who never follows directions

_____

something that looks
delicious but tastes terrible _____

a machine that would
automatically give you a
computerized printout of all
test answers for a given subject _____

an aerosol spray that can
be used to zap an obnoxious
person into an invisible state
(temporarily, of course!) _____

an instrument that could
measure whether or not
a person is in love _____

a long-awaited event that
turns out to be a big
disappointment _____

Meet with a small group of classmates, share your new words, and try to guess which definition each fits. Then work together as a group to create at least five new manufactured words and five real words you think will not be recognized by your classmates. Trade lists with other groups. See if they can identify the real words. Be prepared to provide the dictionary definitions of the words as proof!

Name _____ Date _____

Personal Perspective

CONTENT AREA: Language/Writing

PREPARATION:
1. Each storystarter strip on the supplemental page presents a "character" caught in a perplexing situation. Cut the strips apart.
2. Divide students into small groups. Give each group a copy of the "Personal Perspective" card below. Assign one storystarter to each group.
3. Direct students to read the storystarter aloud and then use it to write individual first-person stories imagining they are the characters. Have them tell how they would feel and what they would do.
4. Provide time for sharing completed stories in the small groups.

a grandmother at a rock concert

Personal Perspective

1. Use the storystarter to write a first-person story. Imagining that you are the character, tell how you would feel and what you would do.
2. Select as a class the one most creative story to be displayed on the class bulletin board.

Personal Perspective

a ragged sock in a fancy suede boot

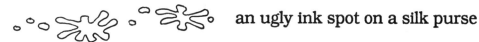 an ugly ink spot on a silk purse

a grandmother at a rock concert

 a fussy teenager at a rain-soaked camp-out

a garden worm caught in a pile of spaghetti

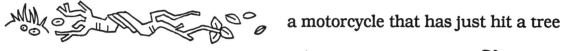 a motorcycle that has just hit a tree

a punker at a preppie party

 a CD that has been played 1,000 times

a teacher accidentally locked in the classroom overnight

 a squirrel in a nut shop

a goldfish out of its bowl

 a birthday cake with 96 lighted candles

Exit-Out

Draw an **X** through the word in each group that does not belong.

1. beef   veal   fish   pork   lamb
2. frolic   gambol   frisk   chance   romp
3. Tennessee   Michigan   Maine   Idaho   Florida
4. cardinal   henna   vermilion   red   crimson
5. badminton   tennis   racquetball table tennis volleyball
6. Georgia   Texas   Alabama   Arizona   Iowa
7. hideous   gruesome   repulsive   countenance homely
8. amateur   judge   connoisseur epicure   critic
9. invertebrate tipsy   bibulous   inebriate   intemperate
10. epigraphy   stenography calligraphy paleography topography
11. submissive ambitious   approach   irrelevant addition
12. Tom   Bob   John   Sue   Ann

Now that you have the idea, use the space below to create five or six EXIT-OUT word groups of your own.

_____

_____

_____

_____

_____

_____

Then meet with a group of classmates, share your individual lists, and choose what you believe to be the most difficult or "trickiest" five of all those your group has created. Contribute these to a class super list and enjoy watching classmates struggle to discover the correct EXIT-OUT words!

Name _____ Date _____

Language/Word Meaning
© 1991 by Incentive Publications, Inc., Nashville, TN

Body Language

There are many words associated with the human body that are also associated with other things. For instance, a bed has both a head and a foot, a river has a mouth, and another name for a computer is a brain. Brainstorm with your partner or small group to discover as many associations as possible for each label below. Be ready to explain your answers to the class.

HEAD

BRAIN

EYE

MOUTH

NECK

CHEST

HEART

STOMACH

ARTERY

HAND

FINGER

MUSCLE

LEG

FOOT

BONUS: A life-size version of the human body may be adapted from this figure and displayed in the classroom where all groups may add their associated ideas.

Name _____   Date _____

Language/Word Association, Meaning
© 1991 by Incentive Publications, Inc., Nashville, TN

*Answer Key

In Defense Of A Chair

This is a chair!

No, this is
a chair.

No, this is a chair.

No, this is
a chair.

What is a chair? Is it a piece of
furniture on which one sits?
Well, then this could be a chair! →
No?

Then, what is a CHAIR?

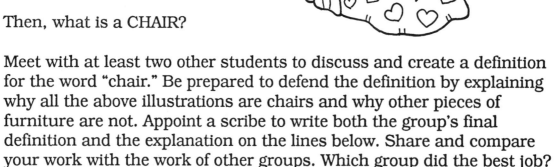

Meet with at least two other students to discuss and create a definition
for the word "chair." Be prepared to defend the definition by explaining
why all the above illustrations are chairs and why other pieces of
furniture are not. Appoint a scribe to write both the group's final
definition and the explanation on the lines below. Share and compare
your work with the work of other groups. Which group did the best job?

_____

_____

_____

_____

Name _____ Date _____

Language/Explicit Definition
© 1991 by Incentive Publications, Inc., Nashville, TN

Zany Authors

Read these directions aloud to yourself.

Have you read the book entitled *The Lost Correspondent* by Willie Everight? How about *Run for Your Life* by T. Rufus Falling? (Get it? If not, reread the paragraph.)

Below are 10 authors. Read their names carefully, and write an appropriate title for each one.

_____ by Ewell C. Gosts

_____ by U. R. Covert

_____ by I. Cara Lott

_____ by B. A. Moron

_____ by Willie Takit

_____ by M. Ike Razy

_____ by Lord Howitt Hurtz

_____ by Lou C. Goosey

_____ by Ima Lone

_____ by Oshee Bledsoe

Now, make up some titles and authors of your own. Meet with a group of 5 or 6 classmates. Share all your titles and authors. Then by democratic process, choose the three most clever titles for your group to share with the entire class.

_____ by _____

_____ by _____

_____ by _____

_____ by _____

Name _____   Date _____

Say It With Words

Can you read these words and phrases? Translate them, and write your answers in the spaces below.

1. BUSH (with arrows forming BEAT around it)

2. ONCE a TIME

3. A B C D E F G H I J K □ M N O P . . . (candy cane)

4. MEAL (M E A L in a box)

5. SIDE SIDE

6. BOOTS PUSS (on a boot)

7. MAN BOARD

8. OUT

9. U JUST me

10. Night / Day (with moon, star, sun)

11. I'm myself

12. BAN ANA (bananas)

1. _____   7. _____
2. _____   8. _____
3. _____   9. _____
4. _____   10. _____
5. _____   11. _____
6. _____   12. _____

Work in groups of three to compare and check your answers. Then create together four or five additional word puzzles similar to these. Trade with other working groups to solve and enjoy!

Name _____   Date _____

Language/Rebus Word Play
© 1991 by Incentive Publications, Inc., Nashville, TN

*Answer Key

Word Power

CONTENT AREA: Language/Values

PREPARATION:
1. Divide students into groups of four or five.
2. Provide felt-tips pens and construction paper for each student.

PROCEDURE:
1. Assign a content area topic of significance to the class for discussion, e.g., protecting endangered species, world peace, improving school spirit, space exploration, etc.
2. Ask each student to think of six words in the English language that could best carry a message to the nation about this subject. The words should then be written on the construction paper and beside each word, the reason for its choice.
3. Have students make posters reflecting their thoughts and chosen words on the subject.
4. After all words and reasons have been shared, direct the groups to carry on a discussion session during which they must choose the individual poster that they consider most powerful.
5. Reassemble the class, and discuss the poster selected by each group. Display all posters on a bulletin board to provoke further discussion.

Personality Parade

CONTENT AREA: Language/Artistic Expression

PREPARATION:
1. Provide felt-tip pens, construction paper, string, and scissors for each student.

PROCEDURE:
1. Ask students to consider personal traits and abilities.
2. Work together in small groups to list as many of these as possible on the chalkboard.
3. Then ask each student to choose one positive quality and one negative quality especially characteristic of his or her personality.
4. Direct students to select one or more colors that represent or express the essence of their positive qualities, and use these colors to create three-dimensional designs that suggest that quality. An example could be joyful, exuberant.
5. Repeat the same process for the negative quality. An example could be fearful, timid.
6. Students then reconvene in small groups to compile composite personality evaluations of the groups and create mobiles to represent qualities of the group as a whole.
7. Hang completed mobiles from the ceiling or on a bulletin board.

For Good Measure

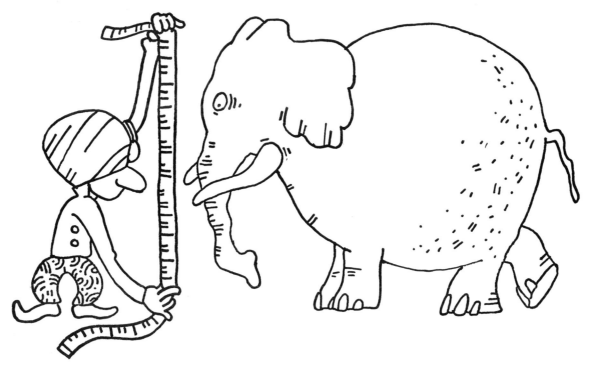

CONTENT AREA: Math/Measurement

PREPARATION:
1. Read aloud to the students the story "The Blind Men and the Elephant."

PROCEDURE:
1. Discuss how blindness causes each man to approach the elephant with a distorted frame of reference.
2. Ask students to conjecture ways in which they could describe objects which could not be handled or felt to persons who cannot see (for example: a train, an acre, features of a person, a large monument, a lion, etc.).
3. Divide students into groups of five or six, and ask them to suppose that there is no uniform system of measurement in existence. Given this problem, each group must devise a new and unique system for measuring height and length that could be used to describe the sizes of buildings, furniture, people, and household objects to someone who has never seen such objects.
4. After the groups have thought of a measurement system, they must plan a demonstration of the use of the new system.
5. Provide time for each group to share results of their thinking and to demonstrate their system.

Logical Links

Each problem on this page is a chain event! Work with a partner to figure out the final link or links in this chain and fill in your answer(s) in the empty space(s). Then give your explanation of the logical progression pattern used in each problem in the space below it.

PATTERN 1: _____

PATTERN 2: _____

PATTERN 3: _____

PATTERN 4: _____

PATTERN 5: _____

Name _____ Date _____

Math/Logic
© 1991 by Incentive Publications, Inc., Nashville, TN

*Answer Key

Haute Cuisine

CONTENT AREA: Math/Money

PREPARATION: Collect menus from several restaurants.
Create or use commercially-made play money.

PROCEDURE:
1. Divide the class into groups of three or four. Appoint a "waiter" for each group.
2. Seat each group around a table and give each group member and each waiter approximately $20-$30 in different denominations of bills and change. Provide menus for each table and ask students to pretend to order a restaurant meal.
3. Ask each student to decide what he or she will order. The waiter for each group must take the order and record the cost of each item, add the sales tax for your city, and total the bill.
4. Each group must then figure the tip on the bill and decide how much each member owes for his or her food plus his or her share toward tax and tip. Members must then decide how to use the money each has available to contribute to the total, making change among themselves to pay as near the correct total as possible.
5. Each group gives the money to the waiter who then takes his or her tip and gives back the proper change if needed.

People Problems

Angelo	Christina	Frederick	Jamie	Melinda	Heather
4 $\frac{1}{3}$ ft.	4 $\frac{1}{2}$ ft.	3 $\frac{9}{10}$ ft.	2 $\frac{5}{8}$ ft.	7 $\frac{1}{8}$ ft.	5 $\frac{1}{2}$ ft
33 $\frac{1}{2}$ lbs.	50 $\frac{2}{10}$ lbs.	30 $\frac{1}{8}$ lbs.	22 $\frac{1}{2}$ lbs.	180 $\frac{3}{4}$ lbs.	95 $\frac{7}{8}$ lbs.

See if you can create some "People Problems." Use the facts written below each of these six people to make up problems on a separate sheet of paper using mixed numerals. In each problem you write, use at least two of the mixed numeral facts above.

Sample problems:

How much more does Heather weigh than Angelo?

Which two people stacked on top of one another would equal exactly the height of Melinda?

Create at least five problems. Write them neatly on another sheet of paper. Solve each problem for yourself on a separate sheet of paper so that you have an answer key with the correct solutions.

Now meet with a group of four or five classmates. Trade papers and try to solve each other's problems. Each may use his or her answer key to check the other's work.

Together We Measure

CONTENT AREA: Math/Measurement

PREPARATION: You will need a postal or food scale, a bathroom scale, measuring cups, and rulers or measuring tapes.

For each student group:
- 1 box (any size)
- 1 rock (any size)
- 1 length of yarn or string
- 1 bottle (any size)
- 1 sack of beans (any kind)
- 1 copy of the student work sheets
  parts 1 and 2 per student

PROCEDURE:
1. Divide the class into small groups.
2. Distribute the above list of materials to each group.
3. Ask students to work together as a group following instructions on the work sheets to answer questions and solve problems.

Together We Measure
Page 1

Work with a small group to complete this activity.
Before you begin to work, read through this entire page carefully.
Use your collective knowledge and energy to solve the problems and
answer the questions. Then write an explanation of **how** you arrived at
your answer.

Find the volume of the space inside this box.

Answer: _____

Explanation: _____

_____

Use a dry measure to estimate the amount of
beans this box would hold.

Answer: _____

Explanation: _____

_____

What is the total outside surface area of this box?

Answer: _____

Explanation: _____

_____

What is the exact weight of your rock?

Answer: _____

Explanation: _____

_____

Name _____ Date _____

Together We Measure
Page 2

What is the exact length of your string?

Answer: _____

Explanation: _____

_____

What is the total amount of liquid that can be held by your bottle?

Answer: _____

Explanation: _____

_____

Which is heaviest - the box of beans, the rock, or the bottle of water?

Answer: _____

What is the total weight of all three? Answer: _____

Which is longest - the string or the total of all outside edges of the box?

Answer: _____

Which has the most volume - the box or the bottle? Answer: _____

Each group member should be able to support answers and explanations. As each approves the final copy, he or she should sign at the bottom of the page.

Approved and signed by:

_____

_____

_____

Name _____ Date _____

GEO-Posters

CONTENT AREA: Math/Plane Geometry – Figures & Angles

PREPARATION: You will need colored construction paper, scissors, paste or glue, rulers, compasses, poster-size tagboard (1 per group).

Write the following words on a chalkboard or chart:

angle	right angle	quadrilateral
trapezoid	obtuse angle	isosceles triangle
parallelogram	circle	acute angle
line segment	rectangle	diameter
parallel lines	ellipse	
equilateral triangle	square	

PROCEDURE:
1. Divide students into groups of three or four.
2. Provide space and the designated materials for each group.
3. Ask individual students to use the materials to create a variety of plane geometric figures.
4. Then ask each group to use the plane figures to create a GEO-POSTER that demonstrates every item listed on the chart or chalkboard.
5. Display the completed posters and ask groups to evaluate one another's work.

Bargain Business

CONTENT AREA: Math/Figuring Discounts

PREPARATION: Prepare cardboard signs that say:

1/3 off	**50% off**
25% off	**1/2 off**
20% off	**30% off**

Provide price tags and felt-tip pens.

PROCEDURE:

1. Divide the class into six groups.
2. Ask each student to contribute an object that can be offered for "sale"– just pretend! (Items can include books, clothing, school supplies, jewelry, etc.)
3. Each group of students must display their sale items on a table and decide a fair market value for each item. Then they must place a price tag on each item.
4. Place one of the cardboard discount sale signs at the center of each table. The group at the table must compute the worth of their items at the discount price, but they should keep these reduced prices a secret.
5. Now all students can become shoppers; they may move around the six tables. Each student must make a wish list of at least eight items he or she would like to purchase. On paper, he or she lists the item name, the retail price, and the discount. He or she returns to his or her own seat to figure the discount prices on all items.
6. When everyone has "shopped," all groups may post their discount prices, and students may check their calculations.

What's Cookin'?

CONTENT AREA: Math/Multiplying & Dividing Mixed Numbers

PREPARATION: Make copies of several recipes for foods that can be easily made and enjoyed by students.
Make enough copies of the WHAT'S COOKIN'? work sheet for everyone.

PROCEDURE:

1. Distribute copies of the WHAT'S COOKIN'? work sheet, and work as a class to begin the process of reducing the recipe to 1/3 of its original amount. Allow students to finish the process independently.
2. Divide students into small groups and give each group a new recipe. Ask them to decide how it needs to be reduced to feed just their small group and to make the necessary changes.
3. Then ask the group to multiply the recipe to feed the entire class.
4. When all groups have completed their tasks, ask each to prepare and present a TV ad for their recipe and allow the class to vote on one they would most like to make.
5. Let the class plan how ingredients will be obtained, and make arrangements to create the recipe for all to enjoy.

What's Cookin'?

Two students are getting ready to make "Granny's Great Granola," but they do not need nearly as much granola as the recipe makes. They want to make only 1/3 of Granny's recipe.

On your own paper or on a recipe card, rewrite Granny's recipe giving the new amounts the students will need.

Granny's Great Granola

4 c uncooked oatmeal	1 $\frac{1}{2}$ c shelled sunflower seeds
$\frac{1}{2}$ c sesame seeds	$\frac{3}{4}$ c wheat germ
1 $\frac{1}{2}$ c shredded coconut	1 $\frac{1}{4}$ c vegetable oil
1 $\frac{1}{3}$ c honey or molasses	2 t cinnamon
	1 $\frac{1}{2}$ c raisins

Measure all ingredients (except raisins) into a large mixing bowl.

Stir until all ingredients are well-coated with liquid.

Spread mixture out into a pan and bake at 300° for $\frac{1}{2}$ hour.

Store mixture in airtight container.

Why don't you take this recipe home and try it?
It's gr-r-r-reat granola. Granny guarantees it!

Nut Crackers

CONTENT AREA: Science/Observation, Research

PREPARATION:
1. Divide class into groups of 3-5 students.
2. Provide each group a collection of four to six different kinds of whole nuts, placed in a see-through container large enough so that each nut can lie flat in the bottom of the container without touching any other nuts. Use peanuts, pecans, hickory nuts, hazelnuts, English walnuts, black walnuts, macadamia nuts, pistachio nuts, etc. (The number of nuts used should be determined by students' ability levels.)
3. In a group discussion, ask the students to look carefully at the nuts in the container and describe each nut as completely as possible. They may discuss similarities and differences, names of nuts, colors, shapes, etc. (At this point, the nuts should not be removed from the container.)
4. When the group has offered all initial observations and ideas, the nuts may be cracked and spread on a table for further study.
5. Place the following study guide, some writing paper, and pens and pencils on the table with the nuts. Add two or three good reference books, or grant library privileges.
6. Using the study guide, students should then use their collected knowledge and resources to write an individual report on each nut.

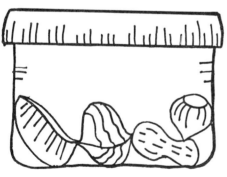

Nut Crackers
Study Guide

1. Take one nut at a time from the container and examine it carefully. Write the name of the nut on another sheet of paper if you know it. If not, leave a space for the name to be filled in later. List the features that are immediately evident to you and the things that you know about the nut.

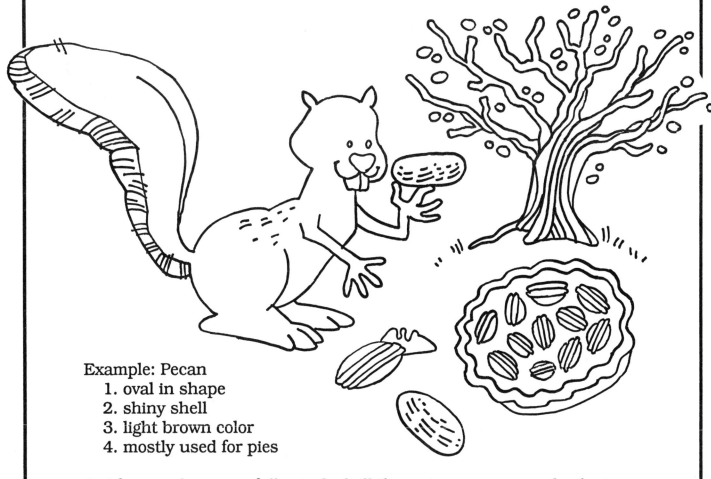

Example: Pecan
   1. oval in shape
   2. shiny shell
   3. light brown color
   4. mostly used for pies

2. After you have carefully studied all the nuts, use resource books to locate specific factual information about each nut. Find out:
- where the nut grows
- how it's grown (on trees, bushes, underground)
- if it grows wild or is cultivated
- how it is harvested
- how it is marketed
- chief uses

Sticky Subjects

CONTENT AREA: Science/Magnetic Attraction

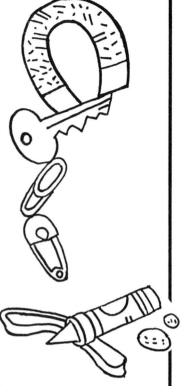

PREPARATION:

1. Prepare and distribute the STICKY SUBJECTS work sheet.

2. Provide:
- Magnets to enable students to work as partners or in small groups during the discussion period.
- An assembly of objects for experimentation. Include some that are magnetic and some that are not. (Object examples include: paper clips, rubber bands, pebbles, safety pins, crayons, keys, etc.)
- Pieces of thin cardboard or heavy construction paper cut to fit maze work sheets.

PROCEDURE:

1. Discuss magnetic attraction. Reinforce the concept that a magnet is able to attract only objects made of metal. Ask students to name objects that will "stick" to a magnet. Discuss ways in which magnets are helpful in daily life. Experiment with the magnets and assembled objects.

2. Divide students into working groups of four or five and instruct each group to:

    a. Spend 5 minutes "cleaning" the classroom with "clean-up" magnets to find objects that could be removed from the setting by magnetism. (Extend the activity outside the classroom if the situation permits.)

    b. Record the information and estimate the size magnet required for each object. (If a 4" magnet can remove paper clips, about how much larger would the magnet have to be to remove a file cabinet?)

    c. Choose 3 objects found in the magnetic cleanup which are small enough to fit in the identified spaces on the STICKY SUBJECTS work sheet.

    d. After attaching cardboard or construction paper to the back of the maze, use a magnet to work the maze to move all the items to the trash can.

3. Reassemble the total group and list items found in the "magnetic cleanup."

    a. Compare information discovered by small groups, and allow time for discussion related to estimation data.

Sticky Subjects

Use a magnet to work the maze to move all the items to the trash can.

START

Magnetic Trash

Name _____ Date _____

Science/Magnetic Attraction
© 1991 by Incentive Publications, Inc., Nashville, TN

41

*Answer Key

Exactly Alike

CONTENT AREA: Science/Symmetry

PREPARATION: Prepare and distribute work sheet.
Provide appropriate art supplies.

PROCEDURE:
1. Explore the concept of symmetry with the entire class. Place your hands together to show how the right hand covers the left and mirrors it. Fold and cut a piece of paper in half to show how one side exactly matches the other. Define symmetry by showing shapes, drawings, or objects that when divided exactly in half, mirror one another perfectly.
2. Divide students into groups of four or five and instruct each group to:
   a. Spend five minutes looking around the classroom to locate objects that when divided in half would be symmetrical. (Examples include: clock, book, map, desk, chalkboard, window, etc.)
   b. Spend another five minutes listing things in nature that are symmetrical. (Examples include: snowflakes, apples, oranges, some leaves and seeds, etc.) If time permits, actually cut these objects in half for illustration.
   c. Fold paper shapes in half to create symmetrical patterns by cutting on both folded and open edges. Separate the two pieces and tape or paste them side by side to form a symmetrical design.
3. Reassemble the total group to share findings and discuss and compare work sheets and designs. Display designs by adding thread to create window or ceiling hangings.
An extended fun activity for identifying lines of symmetry would be to use all the letters of the alphabet and numbers 1-20 for a timed symmetry hunt.
If weather permits, take a symmetry hunt outside and collect symmetrical leaves. Make a mural or scrapbook of your class collection.

Exactly Alike

Circle the drawings that can be symmetrical, and draw the line or lines of symmetry. Then add three drawings of your own.

Your Own Drawings: (Use your ruler if necessary.)

Name _____ Date _____

Mastering Matter

CONTENT AREA: Science/Classifying Matter

PREPARATION:
- Prepare and distribute work sheet.
- Provide poster board or mural paper and art supplies.
- Provide magazines, catalogs, and newspapers for illustration purposes.

PROCEDURE:

1. Define matter as anything that takes up space and has weight. Discuss the three groups of matter:
- Things that do not change their shape when moved are called solids. (A pencil is an example.)
- Things that change their shape when moved or take on the shape of their container are called liquids. (Water is an example of a liquid.)
- Things that have no shape of their own are called gases. (Air in a balloon is a gas.)

2. Divide students into groups of four or five and instruct each group to:
- a. Work together to classify the drawings illustrating matter on the work sheet.
- b. Locate in magazines, catalogs, and newspapers good examples of each classification of matter.
- c. Create a poster divided into three sections labeled: SOLID, LIQUID, and GAS. Use the poster to exhibit pictures cut from the periodicals. (Student drawings may be substituted if other materials are not available.)

3. Reassemble the total class and share completed posters. Display the posters to "spark" further discussion and investigation.
An extension of this activity could be a discussion and illustrations of how matter forms can be changed, e.g., water into ice, flour and water, sugar into liquid, candle or crayon heated, water boiled becomes steam, etc.

Mastering Matter

Matter is anything that takes up space and has weight.

Solids do not change shape when moved.
Liquids change shape when moved and conform to the shape of their container.
Gases do not have a shape of their own.

Write "S", "L", or "G" beside each drawing to show whether it illustrates a solid, liquid, or gas.

Add one example of your own for each form of matter.

Your Own Drawings:

Name _____ Date _____

Listen Here!

CONTENT AREA: Science/Environmental Awareness

PREPARATION: Provide art supplies for murals.

PROCEDURE:
1. Discuss the implications of using good listening habits in daily life.
2. Ask students to name sounds they remember hearing today, on the way to school, in the school building, and in the classroom.
3. Divide students into working groups of four or five and instruct each group to:
   a. Take a five-minute walk through the school building or around the playground (whichever is most appropriate for your situation).
   b. Make notes that include: 1) the names of the individual sounds heard during the walk, and 2) the origin or purpose of each sound (e.g., man-made, animal, weather; to move, to tell time, to signal danger, to communicate ideas, etc.).
   c. Return to the classroom and compile notes, classify the sounds heard, and make one composite record of all the sounds noted.
   d. Work together to make a mural portraying the sounds and their classifications.
4. Reassemble the total class and combine all murals into one display to encourage individuals and groups to compare, contrast, and extend awareness of sounds in the daily environment.

The Real You

This is an opportunity to create a peculiar sort of autobiography without writing a paper! Use a large sheet of drawing paper to create a poster using pictures only (no words) to show some of the following things:

- a self-portrait
- a favorite book or magazine
- your favorite cassette tape or CD
- a list of characters from a favorite TV show
- a box top or label from your favorite food (or a tasty sample)
- an accessory that is you (e.g., belt, hat, sock, shoe, jewelry, scarf, etc.)
- a cartoon that represents your style of humor
- a personal treasure
- your favorite sport
- something you do that makes you proud
- anything that you feel represents the real you

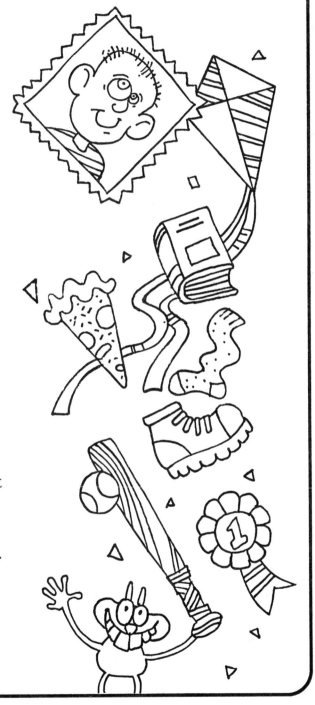

1. Display your completed poster on your desk.
2. Visit the displays of your classmates and discuss what you have learned about each other.
3. Ask classmates to tell you which part of your poster most accurately represents your personality. What have you learned about yourself?
4. Finally, decide which student in your class best represents his or her personality through this medium.

Name _____ Date _____

Shopper's Special

Page 1

CONTENT AREA: Social Studies/Economics

PREPARATION:
1. Set aside classroom space for a "Shopper's Special" learning center.
2. Place in the center the list from which learning activities may be selected. (Enlarge on a poster or laminate several copies of SHOPPER'S SPECIAL *Learning Activities For the "Shopper's Special" Center.*)

PROCEDURE:
1. Introduce the center with a class discussion focused on wise spending and the need for careful buying. List on the chalkboard ideas presented for saving money and receiving full value for money spent for consumer goods and services. Try to direct the discussion to immediate concerns of the students, taking into account spending patterns and life-styles relevant to the group.
2. Ask students to help compose a list of objectives for the center. Make a chart stating these objectives.

3. Ask one group of students to collect empty food containers to be used in the center.

Ask another group of students to accept responsibility for collecting empty prescription medicine bottles, pill boxes, cardboard containers, and other health aid product packages.

A third group of students may be asked to bring labels from clothing, fabric, and leather products. In many instances, the labeled items will need to be brought because of the impracticality of removing the labels.

A fourth group may collect containers for household, automobile, and recreational cleaning supplies.

4. Involve the students in developing criteria for selecting items for the collection:
   ...only empty, clean containers or items
   ...no jagged or rough edges
   ...all labels intact and legible
   ...fits assigned category
   ...permission from parent or guardian for use of the container or item

Emphasize and discuss the importance of collecting items with the stated center objectives in mind, not just randomly picking up the first label or container available.

5. Ask small groups or pairs of students to select at least three activities from the learning center and complete the proper investigations, preparing a brief written or oral report of their findings to share with the class.

Shopper's Special

LEARNING ACTIVITIES FOR THE "SHOPPER'S SPECIAL" CENTER

1. Compare labels of two different brands of food products (fruits, vegetables, cereal, coffee, tea, shortening, eggs). Determine which is the better buy and tell why.
2. Check labels to determine if all important information regarding use and care of the item is given.
3. Check labels for advertising "gimmicks." Question the accuracy and influence of such gimmicks.
4. Compare packages and discuss the additional cost of an item due to packaging. Question the actual worth of the package, and think of some less expensive types of packaging.
5. List the different types of materials used in the packages, and discuss the sources and processes involved in production of the package.
6. Select one package from the center and design a more attractive container for it.
7. Create a brand new product. Draw a picture to show it, list its ingredients, and make a label for it.
8. Develop an advertising slogan for selling a product in the Shoppers Center or for a brand new, just-invented product.

A Trip To Be Remembered

Traveling is one of life's most rewarding experiences. Many people who can't actually pack up and go to faraway places become "armchair travelers." They read and dream about the faraway places they'd like to visit.

Knowing where to get the right books, what to look for, and how to locate information are important to the "armchair traveler." It is just as important, however, to know how to organize the information for future use and to take the time to do it. This helps the "armchair traveler" plan more effective trips.

There are many different areas of information you can study to learn about foreign countries. Match the branches of study shown here with the information you could expect to gain from them about any faraway places.

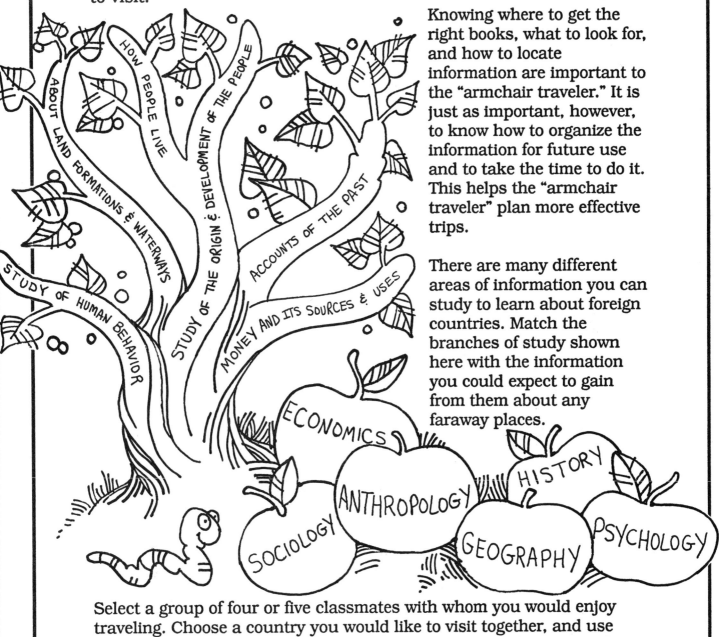

ABOUT LAND FORMATIONS & WATERWAYS

HOW PEOPLE LIVE

STUDY OF THE ORIGIN & DEVELOPMENT OF THE PEOPLE

ACCOUNTS OF THE PAST

STUDY OF HUMAN BEHAVIOR

MONEY AND ITS SOURCES & USES

ECONOMICS

ANTHROPOLOGY

SOCIOLOGY

HISTORY

GEOGRAPHY

PSYCHOLOGY

Select a group of four or five classmates with whom you would enjoy traveling. Choose a country you would like to visit together, and use information from the branches of study to help you plan a one-week trip to be remembered. Show your plan on the ITINERARY FOR "A TRIP TO BE REMEMBERED."

Itinerary For "A Trip To Be Remembered"

Discuss with your group and divide responsibility for making final decisions and plans concerning the following items:

ACCOMMODATIONS: Will you stay in hotels, inns, hostels, or homes? Why?
MONEY: What are the names and denominations of coins and bills used in this country? Value – How does your money convert to this country's currency? Don't forget to set up a budget!
SIGHT-SEEING: What historical sites do you want to include?
Can you intersperse a variety of fun and informative stops on your itinerary?
PEOPLE: What are the best ways to get to know the people and the culture of this country?
TRANSPORTATION: Which is the most efficient and economical transportation for the kind of distance and terrain? Examples are: buses, vans, trains, cars, planes, etc.
FOOD: How will you plan for interesting but economical meals?

	Travel From (city)	Travel To (city)	Means of Transportation	Things to See and Do
Day 1				
Day 2				
Day 3				
Day 4				
Day 5				
Day 6				
Day 7				

Name _____ Date _____

Beautiful Hawaii
Introductory Information

Hawaii is considered by many people to be the most beautiful state in the United States. It is 6,450 square miles in area and is the 47th largest state. It is actually made up of a chain of islands and is the only state in the union completely surrounded by water. The many beaches and miles of warm surf, the moderate temperature, the long hours of sunshine and beautiful sunsets, and the brilliantly colored flowers that bloom year-round have made this state into a tourist spot sought out by people from all over the world.

The 132 islands range in size from the "Big Island" (also named Hawaii) to the tiny uninhabited Kure Island. Trade winds blow from the northeast and were responsible for the routes of sailing ships in days past. It is hard to believe that all these islands were built up by volcanic eruptions over a period of 25 million years.

Main products of Hawaii are: sugarcane, tropical fruits, coffee, macadamia nuts, and fish. Recreation and tourism are the main sources of income for many islanders.

The first settlers were Polynesians who sailed to Hawaii more than a thousand years ago. Since their voyage from distant shores in huge, twin-hulled canoes, their descendants have preserved many of their original traditions. Dances (including the hula), religions, chants, and customs contribute much to the beauty and richness of island life.

Over the years, new arrivals have come to seek their fortunes, build homes, and raise families, so the culture has taken on additional facets and flavors. For this reason, modern Hawaii is sometimes referred to as the "population melting pot of the world."

Beautiful Hawaii
Hawaiian Recall

Read each of the statements below. Color the numbered spaces as directed to find the hidden picture. Choose 1 of the <u>6</u> underlined phrases. Use reference books to research that word or phrase and decide how it relates to Hawaiian life today. Write a paragraph expressing your own ideas on the subject. Meet as a group with other classmates who have written on the same subject. Share your paragraphs and compose together one paragraph including all the important information presented.

1. If Hawaii <u>became a state</u> in 1959, color the #1 spaces light blue.
2. If Hawaii was the 48th state admitted to the United States, color the #2 spaces purple.
3. If Hawaii is the only state in the United States completely surrounded by water, color the #3 spaces dark blue.
4. If the largest island in the Hawaiian chain is Kure, color the #4 spaces pink.
5. If Hawaii is <u>made up of 132 islands</u>, color the #5 spaces light blue.
6. If a chief source of income in Hawaii is <u>tourism</u>, color the #6 spaces brown.
7. If some citizens of Hawaii are <u>descendants of the early Polynesians</u>, color the #7 spaces green.
8. If potatoes are grown in Hawaii, color the #8 spaces red.
9. If Hawaii is really a chain of islands, color the #9 spaces dark blue.
10. If "Hawaii" means "little island," color the #10 spaces purple.
11. If the <u>islands were built by volcanic eruptions</u>, color the #11 spaces yellow.
12. If sugarcane is grown in Hawaii, color the #12 spaces green.
13. If the early Polynesians sailed to Hawaii in triple-hulled canoes, color the #13 spaces red.
14. If trade winds blow over Hawaii from the northeast, color the #14 spaces brown.
15. If Hawaii has a cold <u>climate</u>, color the #15 spaces orange.

Name _____   Date _____

Social Studies/Research, Vocabulary
© 1991 by Incentive Publications, Inc., Nashville, TN

Beautiful Hawaii
Factually Speaking

Reread the BEAUTIFUL HAWAII fact sheet. As you read, underline the sentences that contain information you consider especially important in helping you understand the islands and islanders. Use the information sheet, your dictionary, and the map to help you write good definitions for each of the following words or terms.

island – _____

_____

surf – _____

_____

volcanic eruptions – _____

_____

_____

trade winds – _____

_____

twin-hulled canoes – _____

_____

tourism – _____

_____

melting pot – _____

_____

Name _____ **Date** _____

Social Studies/Research, Vocabulary
© 1991 by Incentive Publications, Inc., Nashville, TN

Beautiful Hawaii

Picture Perfect

Use this map and all of the resource information provided in this lesson to write a one-paragraph description of Hawaii that could be included in a fourth or fifth grade geography textbook. Be sure to include only factual information.

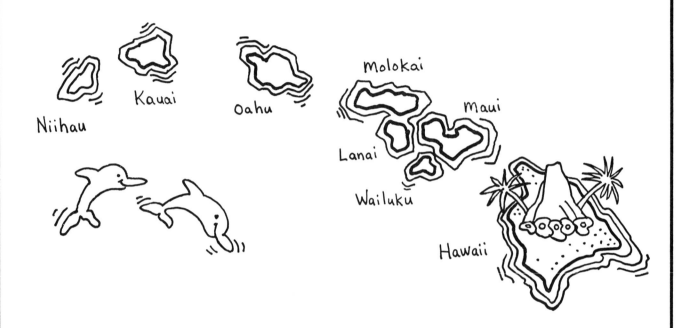

Arrange a group meeting with 3 or 4 classmates. Trade descriptive paragraphs and evaluate each one using the criteria below:
1. Is every statement factual?
2. Is there enough information to provide the reader with a clear geographical picture of the state of Hawaii?
3. Given only the information in this paragraph, could a fourth or fifth grader draw a picture that accurately represents the physical characteristics of a Hawaiian Island?

BONUS: Hawaiian Holiday
Using the collective resources from this lesson and additional information from text and library books, films, magazines, etc., work together as a group to create a travel brochure that would entice tourists to visit one of the Hawaiian islands. Display your brochure in the classroom or library for all to enjoy!

Name _____ Date _____

A Man's A Man For All That

There are many, many labels by which a man or woman may be known: father, mother, banker, artist, friend, critic, aunt, brother, boss, gossip, male, etc. Think of at least as many labels as there are spaces below!

When you have exhausted all your ideas, meet with a small group of classmates, pool your ideas, and make a composite list that includes every possibility you can collectively identify. Share your composite list with the class and discuss the many roles that can be played in one day or in a lifetime by just one person!

Name _____ Date _____

Poll & Pool

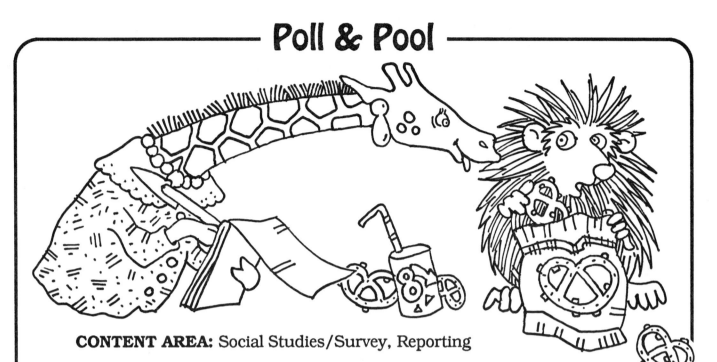

CONTENT AREA: Social Studies/Survey, Reporting

PREPARATION:
1. Write the word "survey" on the chalkboard.
2. In a brainstorming session, ask students to contribute their interpretations of the word and to name the kinds of surveys that come to mind immediately. List all suggestions on the board.
3. Continue the session by discussing ways surveys are made, who makes them, ways in which findings are organized and presented, and who profits from the results of various surveys. Keep the discussion going until all students have had a chance to express ideas.
4. Lead into an individual assignment with a realistic time limit, and give the students the following directions.

PROCEDURE:
1. Select one of the following topics.
   - (1) communicable diseases students in the class have had
   - (2) the least favorite food served in the school cafeteria
   - (3) changes taking place in the neighborhood or school
   - (4) the favorite period of the school day
   - (5) the number of out-of-school hours spent outside by members of the class
   - (6) the number of library books read per week by members of the class
   - (7) the popularity of various television programs
   - (8) junk food eaten by members of the class
2. Develop a plan for conducting your survey. Put your plan into action, organize the results, and report your findings to the class.

It's A Kid's Life

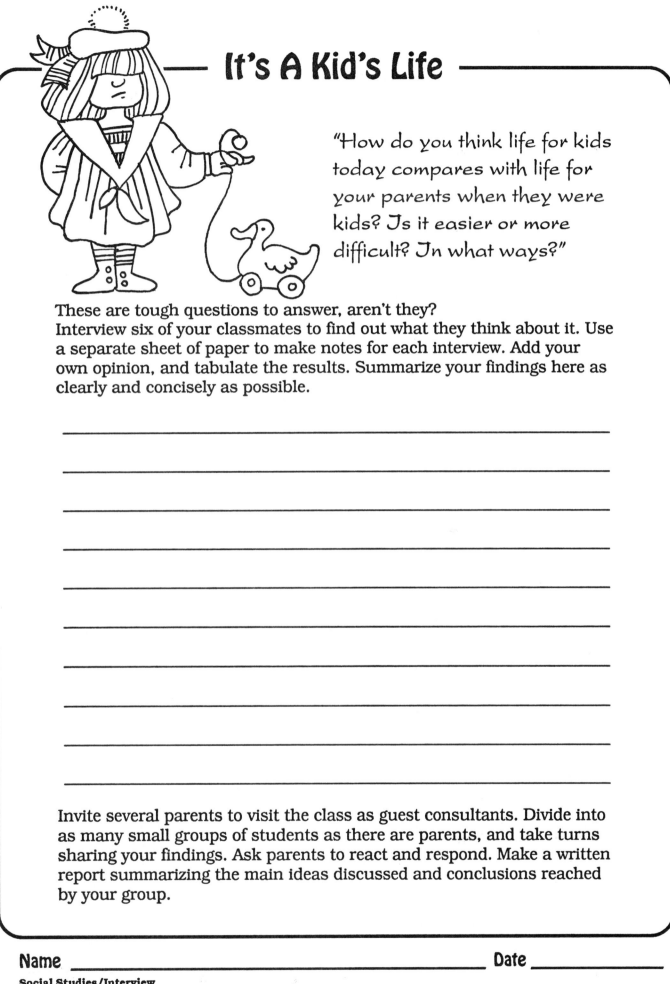

"How do you think life for kids today compares with life for your parents when they were kids? Is it easier or more difficult? In what ways?"

These are tough questions to answer, aren't they?
Interview six of your classmates to find out what they think about it. Use a separate sheet of paper to make notes for each interview. Add your own opinion, and tabulate the results. Summarize your findings here as clearly and concisely as possible.

_____

_____

_____

_____

_____

_____

_____

_____

_____

_____

Invite several parents to visit the class as guest consultants. Divide into as many small groups of students as there are parents, and take turns sharing your findings. Ask parents to react and respond. Make a written report summarizing the main ideas discussed and conclusions reached by your group.

Name _____ Date _____

A Citizen Speaks!

Meet with a group of your classmates to create an appropriate proposal for one of the following changes:

1) A new name for your state
2) A new name for your school
3) A new method for electing a mayor, president, or prime minister
4) A new position in your city, county, state, or national government

Choose one of these and use this form to write your recommendation to the appropriate authority.

To: _____
(Name)

_____
(Address)

_____
(City, State, Zip)

From: _____
(Name)

_____
(Address)

_____
(City, State, Zip)

A Proposal Concerning: _____

_____

_____

Recommendation: _____

_____

_____

_____

Post recommendations on a bulletin board entitled A CITIZEN SPEAKS. When everyone has had an opportunity to read the proposals, discuss and vote to select: (1) the proposal which the class feels is the most worthy, and (2) the proposal which the class feels is most likely to succeed.

Name _____ Date _____

Social Studies/Social. Referendum
© 1991 by Incentive Publications, Inc., Nashville, TN

Criminal At Large

CONTENT AREA: Social Studies/Social Reform

PREPARATION:
1. Provide a sheet of poster-size paper or tagboard for each student.
2. Provide scissors, rulers, pencils, and a variety of colors in paint or crayons.

PROCEDURE:
1. Ask students to work together as a class or in small groups to make a list of persons, places, ideas, emotions, and things that appear to be the cause of some misery in today's world. Some examples are: cancer, greed, littering, prejudice, etc.
2. When the list has been compiled, ask each student to choose one item and design a "wanted" poster to be put in a public place to make people aware of this "criminal."
3. When posters have been completed, provide time for students to show their posters and share with the class a proposal as to what should be done to capture their "criminals."
4. Make arrangements to display posters in the hall or cafeteria where the ideas may be shared with other people.

Nuke Or Not?

Deciding on the best solution to a real-life problem can be very difficult because the alternatives to consider often have both advantages and disadvantages. In order to make the decision that is best and most fair for all concerned, one must weigh the advantages of each alternative against the disadvantages.

One good example of this kind of problem is whether or not a nation should develop the use of nuclear power for domestic purposes.

Listed below are some of the advantages and disadvantages of nuclear power. Use all the resources available to you to add to these lists. (You may wish to subtract some if you find that you disagree with them.)

ADVANTAGES	DISADVANTAGES
1. Nuclear fuel is plentiful.	1. Waste from nuclear must be carefully stored.
2. Nuclear power is clean.	2. Nuclear power can be a threat to national security.

_____

_____

_____

Form a discussion group of classmates who are committed to opposite sides of the issue. Take notes from your discussion to support your position. When you have made as complete an investigation as possible, pretend that you are the person with final authority to make the decision. State your decision, and give your rationale on the lines below.

_____

_____

_____

Name _____ Date _____

Social Studies/Investigation, Decision-Making
© 1991 by Incentive Publications, Inc., Nashville, TN

Sleuth On The Sly

CONTENT AREA: Observing and Recording

PREPARATION:
1. Create a bulletin board or display space entitled SLY OBSERVATIONS.
2. Ask each student to print his or her full name on a strip of paper. Place these strips in a basket or box. Then allow each student to draw a name.
3. Provide the following instructions.

1) Read the name you have drawn to find out which classmate you will observe.
2) For one entire day, secretly observe and record your person's activities. Carefully note time, places, and specific activities.
3) Remember, a good private eye needs to be "undercover" and operate in secrecy. The success of your dectective work will depend on the person being observed not knowing when he or she is being observed or who the observer is!
4) At the appropriate time, place your observation note sheets on the SLY OBSERVATIONS bulletin board.

PROCEDURE:
1. Number each entry on the SLY OBSERVATIONS bulletin board for easy referral.
2. Divide students into groups of four or five.
3. Ask individuals to read the observations carefully and make a note as to their personal guess at the identity of each.
4. They must then meet with their designated groups to discuss their opinions and decide one identity for each entry.
5. Finally, give groups time to share their guesses and tell why and how they arrived at their final opinion.

Facts Worth Filing

CONTENT AREA: Research and Organization – any content area

PREPARATION:

1. Select a topic of interest to the group, one that is out of the ordinary and not specifically related to topics generally studied at your level or locality. Ask students to contribute suggestions for a really exotic topic.

Suggestions:
Sea monsters
Castles
Little people
(dwarfs, pygmies, midgets)
Hobbies of American presidents
Personal idiosyncrasies of world
  leaders

Druids, elves, or leprechauns
Statistics related to the lives of
  teens, rock singers, race car
  drivers, sky divers
Solutions to pollution
Night life under the sea

2. Secure a 5" x 7" card file box and appropriate cards. Label the box "Facts Worth Filing About _____ ." Place the box in a spot convenient to the students.

PROCEDURE:

1. Provide the following study guide.

1. Try to find all the information you can about this topic. Use the library, reference books, magazines, newspapers, brochures, and any other sources.
2. Record the information that you think is valuable and worth saving on cards for the file box. Be sure to give the exact source of your information, including page numbers. Sign your name at the bottom of the card and date it before you file it in the box.

2. At the end of a specified time, elect a committee to sort through the box and pick out the most interesting and informative cards. The committee will also organize the cards and present a report to the group on why these facts were selected as worth remembering.

FOLLOW-UP ACTIVITIES:

1. Come up with a creative way to organize and present the facts for a culminating project — a giant mural, a scrapbook, a party, etc.
2. Each student might select a topic of personal interest and collect "Facts Worth Filing" for an individual project.

Survival Scheme

CONTENT AREA: Multiskill

PREPARATION:
1. Create a SURVIVAL SCHEME learning center. The above illustration may be enlarged to serve as a backdrop for the center. Books and pictures on camping, hiking, and outdoor survival may provide additional motivation.
2. Reproduce appropriate quantities of the student work sheets and add these to the center.
3. Provide paper, pencils, crayons, and other art supplies.

PROCEDURE:
Discuss with students the work procedure for each activity in the entire SURVIVAL SCHEME center. Some tasks will be done individually, others in group settings. (Make small group assignments for group activities.) A suggested plan follows:

- YOU ARE THERE! - individual
- ROLE RELATIONSHIPS - Small groups
- PRESENTING A PLAN ⎫ - Individual followed by small group
- SELECTION LIMITED ⎬ discussion and consensus
- EMOTION INVENTORY ⎭
- SEND THE MESSAGE - Group or individual

Survival Scheme
You Are There!

Four best friends have enjoyed a great day of hiking in a large national forest reserve. Midafternoon, intrigued by some nearby animal noises, they leave the trail and follow the sounds into a dense forest. They have a good chase but never come upon the animal activity. Suddenly, they realize the sun has set and the forest is fast growing dark and cold. Their backpacks carry only a few leftover snacks and half-empty canteens. They are wearing only light jackets and can see no clear exit through the trees and underbrush to a trail or campsite. No one can remember which way he or she entered the forest. Worst of all, you are one of the four, and all of you are tired and scared.

Wisely, you sit down to discuss the matter. One friend feels that it is important for the group to stay together in this very spot and wait for the morning light to guide the way home. Another hiker suggests that you split up and move five minutes in four different directions to explore for a path or familiar landmarks, then return to this spot to make further decisions. The third friend is visibly upset, insecure, and unable to contribute any ideas.

Now the whole group is looking to you for leadership. Shall they follow one of the two proposed plans, or do you have a better idea? Make a list of the pros and cons of each plan. Then tell which plan you feel is the wiser and why.

_____

_____

_____

_____

_____

_____

Name _____ **Date** _____

Survival Scheme
Role Relationships

CONTENT AREA: Problem-Solving, Social Interaction

PREPARATION:

1. Arrange a time and place for students to work in groups of four to role play the situation given in YOU ARE THERE! Discuss the problem, the proposed solutions, and the character implications before groups begin role playing.

For example: One friend suggested a plan, another felt very strongly, a third had absolutely no ideas or suggestions, and the fourth presented a detailed outline. How do you bring this out in role playing?

Is the problem agreeing upon a plan, sticking together, getting out of the forest, or something else? Is it easy to stick to the main topic in role playing?

How does it feel to be in the person's shoes you will represent? Can you really "feel" and "act" with and for that person?

PROCEDURE:

1. Allow ample time for each group to gain the full benefit of the role-playing situation.

2. Gather the total group for an evaluation discussion. Focus on questions such as these.
   - What emotions surfaced during the role playing?
   - How did it feel to be the person with no ideas to share?
   - Did some solutions to the real problem emerge?

3. Wrap up the discussion with an analysis of role playing as a vehicle for creative thinking.

Survival Scheme

Presenting A Plan

Rethink the proposed solutions presented in YOU
ARE THERE! and decide upon a plan of your own.
Your plan may or may not include some portion of
one or both of the other two.
Use a formal outline to explain your plan so that
your friends will understand and accept it.

Name _____ Date _____

Survival Scheme
Selection Limited

Draw pictures of the three items you think would be helpful to the four lost people. Circle the one item you think would be most helpful. Write three sentences to explain why you selected this item as the most helpful and how it would be used.

1. _____

_____

2. _____

_____

3. _____

_____

Name _____ Date _____

Reasoning
© 1991 by Incentive Publications, Inc., Nashville, TN

Survival Scheme
Emotion Inventory

Because you and your friends are faced with a frightening situation and have a difficult choice to make, you will experience various emotions and feelings within a very brief time period.
Circle the emotions and feelings that you would expect to be experienced by some or all members of the group.

ANGER   *Sympathy*   **COURAGE**

GRIEF   FEAR   *Joy*

HAPPINESS   **GENEROSITY**

 # GREED   PATIENCE

ANXIETY   **HOSTILITY**

EXCITEMENT   **FRIENDSHIP**

 *AGGRESSIVENESS*

On a separate sheet of paper, write a paragraph to explain how or under what circumstances these emotions might be expressed. Discuss what would be the most appropriate response(s) to each emotion.

Name _____ Date _____

Projecting, Reasoning
© 1991 by Incentive Publications, Inc., Nashville, TN

Send The Message

CONTENT AREA: Inventing, Combining

PREPARATION:

1. Assemble a box of junk including some of the items
listed plus others to be contributed by students.

- spools
- twine
- paper clips
- paper cups & plates
- bowls, spoons, forks,
  & knives
- spatula
- straws

- bottles
- plastic tablecloth
- jump rope
- foam rubber
- old mirrors
- egg cartons
- scissors
- tape or glue

2. Print the following directions on a study guide and place it beside
the box.

Great Inventions

"Necessity is the mother of invention." Can you explain the
meaning of this famous saying? You can actually illustrate its
meaning by "inventing" a one-of-a-kind, never-seen-before item for
the "Great Inventions Museum."

1. Think about how each item in this box of junk might be used
   together with one or more other items to create an item
   carrying a message about a cause you believe in.
2. Draw a diagram of the completed item, give it a name, and write
   a description of it. Add a sentence about the social message it
   is meant to convey.
3. Add your completed diagram and a description to the GREAT
   INVENTIONS collection.

---

3. Ask students to work in small groups to follow the directions on the
box.
4. After all inventions are completed, reconvene the total group to
discuss and evaluate the "inventions."

A Tour Too Good To Miss!
Page 1

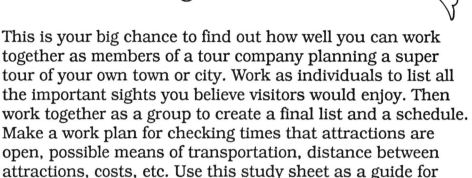

This is your big chance to find out how well you can work together as members of a tour company planning a super tour of your own town or city. Work as individuals to list all the important sights you believe visitors would enjoy. Then work together as a group to create a final list and a schedule. Make a work plan for checking times that attractions are open, possible means of transportation, distance between attractions, costs, etc. Use this study sheet as a guide for planning. Then make your tour schedule and map.

Places to Visit	**What to See**
_____	_____
_____	_____
_____	_____
_____	_____
_____	_____
_____	_____
_____	_____
_____	_____

Method of transportation:_____ **Cost of tour:** _____

Other notes: _____

_____

BONUS: You might create a flier or poster to attract customers and announce some of the highlights of your tour! Your class might even actually take one of the proposed tours!

Name _____ Date _____

A Tour Too Good To Miss!

Page 2

Fill in your tour schedule here.

8:00 a.m. — Coffee, hot chocolate, tour overview

8:30 a.m. — _____

9:00 a.m. — _____

9:30 a.m. — _____

10:00 a.m. — _____

10:30 a.m. — _____

11:00 a.m. — _____

11:30 a.m. — _____

12:00 noon — _____

12:30 p.m. — _____

1:00 p.m. — _____

1:30 p.m. — _____

2:00 p.m. — _____

2:30 p.m. — _____

3:00 p.m. — _____

3:30 p.m. — _____

4:00 p.m. — _____

4:30 p.m. — Tour ends — Farewell and happy memories!

Name _____ Date _____

Planning, Organizing
© 1991 by Incentive Publications, Inc., Nashville, TN

A Tour Too Good To Miss!

Tour Guide Map
Page 3

Use this space to show a map of your tour. Mark the starting place with a star or an X. Trace the route you will take and mark the stops. (You may use a printed map, or create your own.)

When you have traced your route, figure exactly the distance your tour will cover in miles or kilometers.

Name _____ Date _____

Good News And Bad News

CONTENT AREA: Problem-Solving

PREPARATION: None

PROCEDURE:
1. Present GOOD NEWS AND BAD NEWS to the class and lead a discussion of approaches to solving the problem.
2. Divide the class into small discussion groups. Ask each group to devise at least one plan for solving the problem.
3. Reconvene the total group to share solutions and select the one best solution.

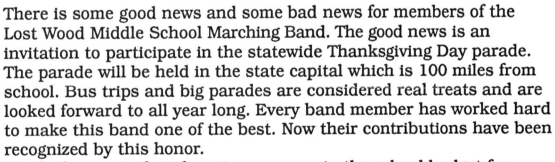

There is some good news and some bad news for members of the Lost Wood Middle School Marching Band. The good news is an invitation to participate in the statewide Thanksgiving Day parade. The parade will be held in the state capital which is 100 miles from school. Bus trips and big parades are considered real treats and are looked forward to all year long. Every band member has worked hard to make this band one of the best. Now their contributions have been recognized by this honor.

The bad news is that there is no money in the school budget for out-of-town trips. The band sponsored a fund-raising drive earlier in the year to make money for new uniforms. Another fund-raising effort is out of the question. The band director has proposed asking community businesses to contribute money for the trip, but the principal is not comfortable with this approach. Many members of the band simply do not have money to contribute for their own expenses. Time is passing quickly and the invitation must be either accepted or declined. Can you think of an acceptable way to raise the money?

Categorically Speaking

The twenty-two objects below could be classified in several different ways. For starters, you might group all "the objects you could lift" together and "the objects too heavy to be lifted" together. "Living things" might make up one group and "nonliving things" another.

Look at all the objects carefully.

On the back of the sheet, list as many new categories for classification as possible.

When you have exhausted your own ideas, meet with three classmates and pool your creative energy to add to your lists.

Be prepared to share and defend your collective lists with the entire class.

Name _____ Date _____

Time Out!

Keep a record of how you spend your time for the next week.

	TV	Meals	Home-work	Sports	Sleep	Work/Chores	Telephone	Leisure Time w/friends & family
Mon.								
Tues.								
Wed.								
Thurs.								
Fri.								
Sat.								
Sun.								
Total								

At the beginning of the next week, meet with a group of classmates to share and compare findings. Tally all information collected by individual members of the group and make a composite record of time spent in each activity.

As a group, make at least five generalizations about how middle graders spend out-of-school time.

Share generalizations with other class groups to see if you have arrived at some of the same conclusions. Discuss any opposing opinions. Also, as a class, discuss any changes that could be made to improve the quality of time expenditure by middle grade students in general.

Name _____ Date _____

Who Has The Button?

CONTENT AREA: Problem-Solving, Logic

PREPARATION: Make one copy of the lower portion this page for each student.

PROCEDURE:
1. Divide students into groups of 3-5. (Try to distribute problem-solving abilities as equally as possible.)
2. Ask student groups to work together to read and solve the problem. Time the groups. See which group can solve the problem most quickly.
3. When all groups have finished, share results and discuss techniques that foster efficiency in group work habits as well as the techniques used to solve the problem. (How were these methods employed by the groups that finished most quickly?)

| Clown | Witch | Boy | Professor | Cop |

Each person above is holding an object which you cannot see.

The 5 objects are:
       an arrow   a button   a bone   a star   a mop

However, they are not in this order.
Given the information below, see if you can figure out which character has the BUTTON!

1. The BONE is not next to the MOP, and neither is the STAR.
2. The STAR is not next to the BUTTON, and neither is the BONE.
3. The MOP is not next to the ARROW, and neither is the STAR.
4. The BUTTON is just to the left of the ARROW.

_____ has the BUTTON!

*Answer Key

Wild Guess

CONTENT AREA: Hypothesizing - any content area

PREPARATION:
1. Divide students into three or four small groups.
2. Locate in books, coloring books, and magazines (or draw) a picture of a "wild thing" for each group.
   A "wild thing" might be something such as:
   - a rock musician with a wild hairstyle.
   - a wild animal.
   - a jungle scene.
   - a traffic jam.
   - a storm.

Make as many copies of each "wild thing" as needed for members of the group.

3. Prepare for each student a cover page of dark construction paper in which holes have been randomly punched. Staple one over each picture page. Secure at top, bottom, and sides so the students cannot see the picture except through the holes in the cover sheet.

PROCEDURE:
1. Distribute the covered picture pages to the students.
2. Explain to the students that an object is pictured on the covered page. Their task is to hypothesize as to what that object might be by looking through the punched holes.
3. Direct students to consider each hole separately, look at each carefully, decide what the object might be if it appears as it looks through that single opening, and write the decision beside the hole.
4. After students have considered each hole and made their guesses, they should review these and make a general hypothesis of what the entire picture is.
5. Students return to their groups to share their hypotheses and combine their ideas to make one hypothesis. When this has been agreed upon, students may tear off the cover sheets to check their hypotheses.

NOTE: The picture pages may be used as motivation for brainstorming, vocabulary extension, and/or springboards to creative writing.

Party Producer

CONTENT AREA: Planning & Organizing

PREPARATION:

1. Write this list on the chalkboard.

Mozart
State of Texas
Golden Gate Bridge
an ant
spring
Peter Rabbit
Sherlock Holmes
Declaration of Independence
the moon
Father Time

a pet rock
your oldest tennis shoe
Mississippi River
Washington Monument
the hit that made the winning run
   in the World Series
a mermaid
Cleopatra
Johnny Appleseed
the first automobile

2. Reproduce a copy of the PARTY PRODUCER work sheet for each student.

PROCEDURE:

1. Tell students you are commissioning each to produce a huge party or event to be given in honor of one of the "personalities" listed above. Each "producer" must plan his or her entire event using the accompanying work sheet as a guide.

2. When plans are complete, divide students into groups of 5 or 6. Each "producer" shares his or her plans within the group. Then the group votes on which party would be the most interesting and exciting to attend.

3. Provide time for the winners from each group to present their plans to the entire class. The class then votes to determine which party would be the most exciting of all.

Party Producer

A Party For _____

Production plans and arrangements by:

_____ Date: _____

Description of Setting or Place for the Party:

Party Theme:

Suggestions for Decorations:

Suggestions for Entertainment:

Suggestions for Food:

Ideas for Invitations:

Special Guests:

Additional Ideas:

Improvement, Inc.

CONTENT AREA: Brainstorming

PREPARATION:

1. Gather one or two objects from the following list for each of 4 or 5 groups of students. (Some groups may wish to supply their own objects.)

ice cream cone	*baseball mitt*
bathroom scales	*alarm clock*
fork	*pencil or pen*
recipe box	*wastebasket*
small jewelry box	*dictionary*
empty billfold	*barrette*
coffeepot	*toothbrush*
white glue bottle	*dollar bill*
tape dispenser	*box of cereal*

2. Reproduce one copy of the following MEMO work sheet for each group.

PROCEDURE:

1. Divide students into four or five groups. Ask each group to appoint a recorder.

2. Direct students to brainstorm ideas for improvements on the object(s) given to their group. The recorder lists all ideas on a sheet of paper.

3. Students then agree on the improvements which should be included on a model drawing of the object as they would present it to the manufacturer. The recorder lists these on the MEMO page, and another student (or students) makes the model drawing in the space provided on the MEMO page.

Improvement, Inc.

Memo

To the manufacturers of : _____

From members of IMPROVEMENT, INC.

_____

_____

_____

Suggestions for improvement of aforementioned object.

1._____   6._____

2._____   7._____

3._____   8._____

4._____   9._____

5._____   10._____

Drawing of object with proposed improvement(s):

Name _____   Date _____

Take A Position

CONTENT AREA: Debating — any content area

PREPARATION:
1. Provide a copy of the TAKE A POSITION work sheet for each student.

PROCEDURE:
1. Direct each student to read the work sheet carefully and determine which position he or she can defend most honestly.

2. Divide the class into two teams of like persuasions. Provide time for teams to meet and discuss their ideas.
3. Ask each team to keep notes on points favoring that side of the issue.
4. Ask each team to appoint two members of the group as representatives to sit on a panel of "expert debators."
5. Stage a debate in which the debators present, refute, and defend their positions.

Take A Position

Yes! Television, as an efficient source of information; a vehicle for vicarious experience; or a smorgasbord of ideas and ideals, makes more of a **positive** than a negative contribution to successful living.

Television, as a "hypnotist of the mind"; a creator of unrealistic goals and desires (especially in advertising); and as a medium which breeds indolence and nonparticipation, makes more of a **negative** than a positive contribution to successful living.

NO!

You must choose to support one of the above statements.

Which will you choose? After you decide, write a paragraph supporting your opinion.

To help you decide, ask yourself these questions:

1. How much time do your family members and you spend watching TV?
2. What are the reasons you watch TV?
3. In what good ways has TV affected your life?
4. What bad effects has TV had on you?
5. In the near future, TV may be used as an instrument for actually looking into your home—asking questions and tabulating your responses. How could that affect your life?

Wish You Were Here

CONTENT AREA: Researching

PREPARATION:
1. Provide stationery, postcards, and brochures from various hotels and resorts. It may take some time to collect all of this, but it makes a nice project for teacher and students. Maybe some friends outside the classroom will also contribute.
2. Add maps, globes, atlases, and reference books appropriate to students' ability and interest levels.
3. Divide students into small groups and provide the following directions for each group.

Place Stamp Here

1. Select one hotel or resort to "visit."
2. Before you write, do the research necessary to help you tell all about the marvelous time you would surely be having if you were there.
3. Use the stationery or postcard from your chosen hotel or resort to write to a friend or relative.
4. Use the brochures, maps, atlases, and resource books to find information to complete the WISH YOU WERE HERE work sheet.

Wish You Were Here

Use atlases, maps, and resource books to find *specific* answers to these questions. Do *not* guess.
Write the full name and address of the hotel or resort you have chosen on the line below.

_____

1. How many actual miles is it from your home to the hotel or resort?

_____

2. Would it be best to travel to your destination by train, car, bus, or airplane? Why?

_____

_____

3. What will be the main type of recreation available to you?

_____

4. What special sports or entertainment equipment do you need to take with you?

_____

5. What kinds of clothes will you need to take?

_____

6. Will your vacation cost be:

cheap _____ average _____ expensive _____

7. Write a brief paragraph on the back of this sheet telling about the scenery you expect to see.

8. List the single most interesting thing you've found out about your vacation spot.

_____

_____

Name _____ Date _____

It's Your Game

Page 1

CONTENT AREA: Planning and Organizing — any content area

PREPARATION:

1. Divide the class into groups of three.

2. Reproduce the game board pages for each group.

3. Provide a manila file folder for each group along with glue, paper, pencils, crayons, felt-tip pens, colored construction paper, scissors, index cards, and envelopes.

4. Discuss and list on the chalkboard the many uses and purposes of an educational game board.

5. Distribute the two halves of the blank game board and the file folders. Make sure the other supplies are accessible to students for free-time use.

6. Provide the instructions listed under "Procedure."

It's Your Game
Page 2

PROCEDURE:

1. Use the materials to design a game to teach or reinforce a specific skill.
2. Plan the entire game, including patterns, dice, tokens, game cards, etc., on scrap paper.
3. Arrange your game board sheets as you wish, and paste them into the folder.

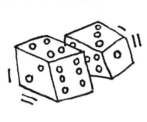

4. Complete the game board by adding directions and illustrations. Use crayons, felt-tip pens, pencils, and/or construction paper cutouts.

5. Make all supporting materials, and place these in an envelope to be clipped inside the game folder.
6. Print the name of the game, the purpose, and rules for playing the game on the outside of the folder.

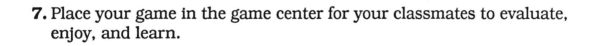

7. Place your game in the game center for your classmates to evaluate, enjoy, and learn.

It's Your Game

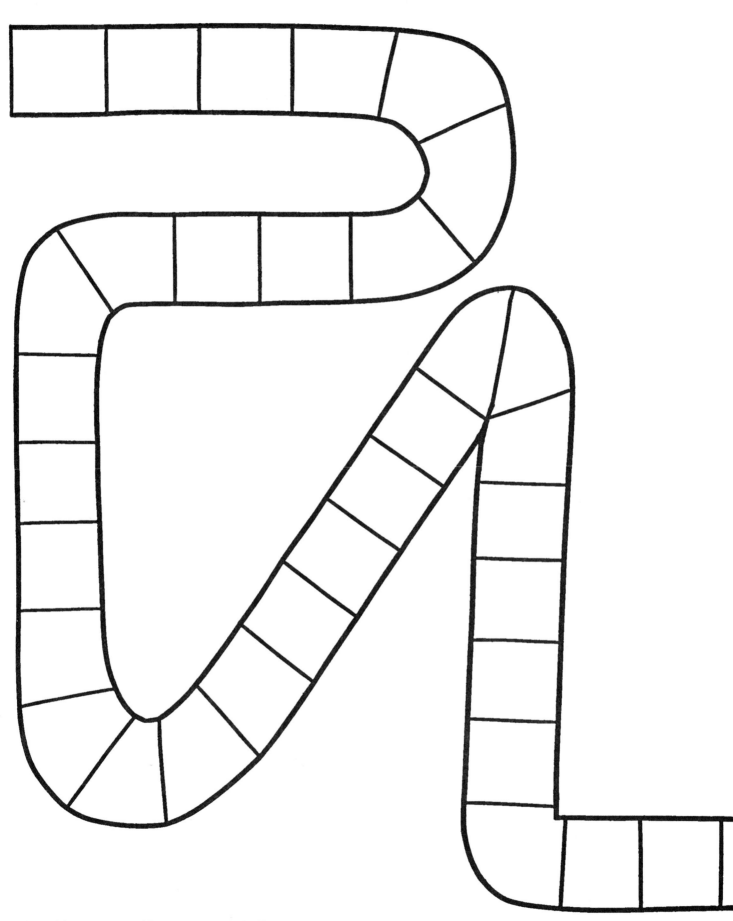

It's Your Game

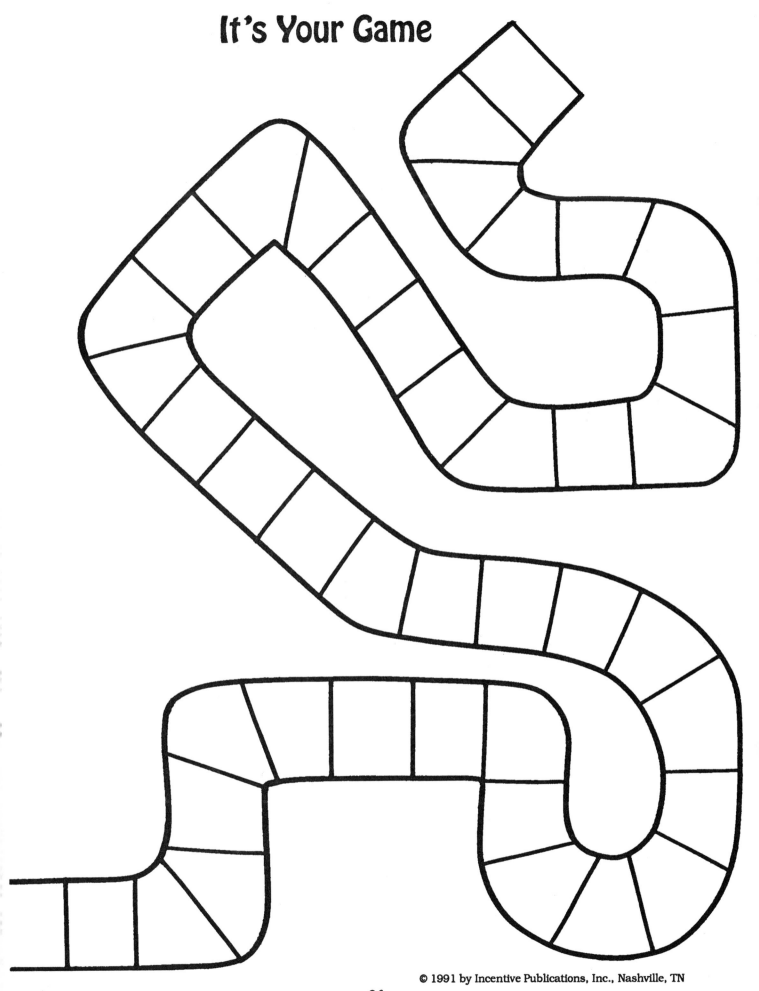

A Better Mousetrap

Work with a small group of classmates to think of ways in which you could combine two or more objects on this page to create a brand new object. Find as many combinations as possible. Draw lines to connect each set of objects you want to combine with a different color fine-tip marker. Appoint one member of your group to describe each new object in a brief paragraph. Another member may illustrate your new invention.

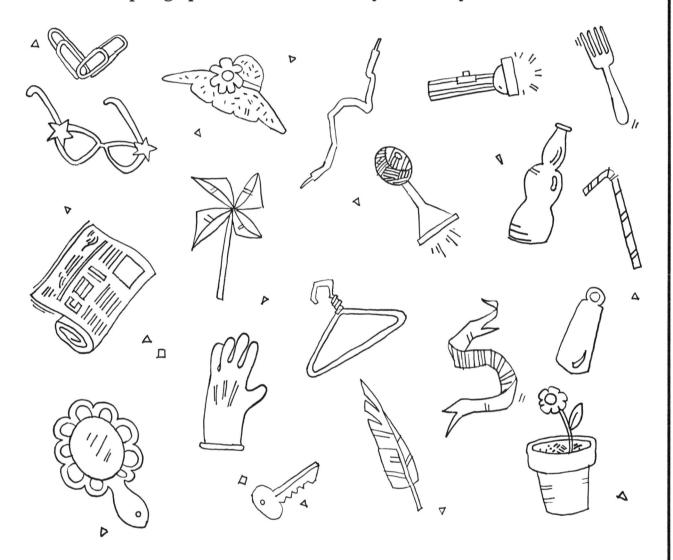

BONUS: As a homework assignment, actually create one or more of your projected ideas, or redo the assignment using a brand new group of objects. Name your new creation and bring it to share with the class.

Name _____ Date _____

Shipwrecked!

Pretend you have been shipwrecked on a small tropical island. Another one of the survivors is a small girl who lost her very favorite toy, a dollhouse, in the shipwreck. You and your friends want to make her happy by creating a temporary dollhouse for her to play with on the island.

The little girl has started a list of things her new house will need. Your job is to find materials to use and ways to put them together to simulate each piece.

1. Together the group must plan a simple layout for the house.
2. Then, each group member should:
    a) Choose from the list one object to make.
    b) Draw a picture of how the object will look when it is finished.
    c) Add labels to tell what island materials will be used for each part.
3. Appoint a group architect. He or she will be responsible for drawing a sketch of the entire house with a place designated for each piece of furniture.
4. Place all completed drawings in a folder so they may be shared with all groups. (You may wish to ask a first grade group of girls to vote for the best dollhouse!)

Information, Please!

CONTENT AREA: Researching

PREPARATION: Make a copy of the INFORMATION, PLEASE! study guide for each student.

Make available library time and/or a wide variety of resources including: telephone directory, dictionary, atlas, catalogs, almanac, encyclopedia, timetables, consumer guide, etc.

PROCEDURE:
1. Divide students into small study groups.
2. Explain that they will have 15 minutes to meet with their group, read the assignment, and make a plan for the most efficient way to gather the information required. Each group will work to complete one study guide.
3. At a signal, the groups may begin their research.
4. Keep track of the order in which groups finish their task.
5. Discuss what knowledge, methods of cooperation, and research techniques were employed that made the problem-solving process efficient. What kinds of things hindered the process?

Information, Please!
Study Guide

FIND OUT...

1. What is the fastest way to get a package from your city to Chicago, Illinois, USA (or if you live in Chicago, the fastest way to Toronto, Ontario CANADA)?

2. Which has the fewest calories: a cheeseburger, fried chicken, or one scoop of ice cream with chocolate syrup?

3. Who created Frankenstein?

4. At what temperature should you cook pork chops?

5. What time can cartoons be seen on TV in your city?

6. What is the best price for 5 pounds of white granulated sugar today?

7. How do you pronounce "lutetium"?

8. Who was awarded the Nobel Peace Prize in 1970?

9. Which has the highest sugar content—apples, oranges, or pears?

10. List books by author Stephen King.

11. What is the average temperature in Japan in April?

12. What was the coldest day in the USA last year?

13. What time does a plane leave from San Francisco, California, to fly to Sidney, Australia, on January 1?

14. What are five famous country music hits of the 60s?

15. When does the first morning bus leave your town for a city approximately 100 miles away?

16. What color is "chartreuse"?

17. What is the abbreviation for the word "route"?

18. What is the cost of a call from Anchorage, Alaska, to Boston, Massachusetts, at 7 p.m. on a Wednesday evening?

19. Who is/was the author of the book *Pinocchio* and what year was it written?

20. What is the time and date in Hong Kong when it is 6 p.m. on September 1 in Halifax, New Brunswick CANADA?

Answer Key

Page 12

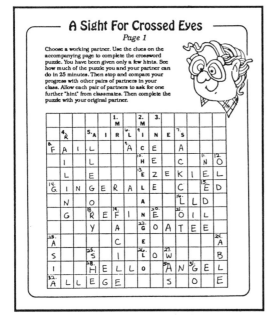

Page 21

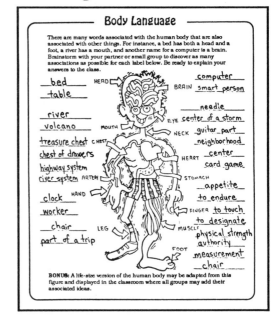

Page 24

1. Beat around the bush
2. Once upon a time
3. Noel
4. A square meal
5. Side by side
6. Puss in boots
7. Man overboard
8. Inside out
9. Just between you and me
10. Turn night into day
11. I'm beside myself
12. Banana split

Page 30

$62\,^3/_8$

Christina & Jamie

Page 78

The witch has the BUTTON!

Page 28

PATTERN 1. 2 consecutive numbers; then skip 1

PATTERN 2. Multiply each product by a consecutive number

PATTERN 3. Plus 2; plus 3; plus 4; plus 5; plus 6; etc.

PATTERN 4. Multiply each number by 2 to get next number

PATTERN 5. Subtract 13 from each number to get next number

Page 41

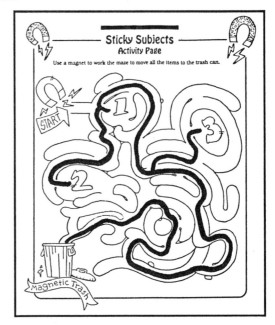